PUZZLE TOWN

Susannah Leigh

Designed and illustrated by
Brenda Haw

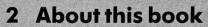

Contents

Series Editor: Gaby Waters

About this book

There's a fancy dress party in Puzzle Town today. Katy and Tim are invited, but they don't know where to find the party.

An exciting trail of clues and puzzles on every double page will lead them to it. See if you can solve them all and help Katy and Tim on their way. If you get stuck you can look at the answers on pages 31 and 32.

Puzzle Town

Tim

Katy

Fancy dress

Here are Katy's and Tim's fancy dress outfits. One piece is hiding on every double page. If you can't spot them all, the answers on page 32 should help you. Can you guess what Katy and Tim are going as?

Face paints

√ Joke flower

√ Cloak

Funny wig

√ Spell book

Big shoes

√ Hat

√ Slippers

√ Red nose

√ Striped socks

√ Wand

√ Magic kitten

2

Party clues

On some pages there are special party clues, like this one. They will help you find the party, so look out for them.

The party pixie

Party pixie

This is the party pixie. He is in charge of the Puzzle Town party. He helps Katy and Tim on the trail by giving them some important instructions to follow. Keep your eyes peeled.

Odd things

Puzzle Town is a very strange place. If you look very carefully, you will see a lot of odd things. See how many you can spot on every double page.

Balloon thief

Someone has stolen the Puzzle Town party balloons. The thief is hiding on every double page. Can you spot the balloons he has taken?

Setting off

The day of the Puzzle Town party was sunny and bright. Katy and Tim set off on their trail. In their hands they held a letter from the party pixie.

"First let's work out which Puzzle Town shops we need to go to," said Tim, looking at the letter. "The quicker we do, the quicker we'll find the party."

Which shops must Tim and Katy go to? Can you spot them?

Dear Katy and Tim,
  Before you set off on the trail of the Puzzle Town party, here are a few things you must do.
  Love from the Party Pixie x x x

Buy some cakes for the party

Get some party hats

Buy party fruit

Collect Katy's new shoes

Post letters

P.S. There are clues along the way and an invitation at the end of the trail. Good luck!

Butcher

Baker's Shop

Lovely cakes

Katy and Tim raced off to the bakers. Here they found some of the most delicious looking cakes they had ever seen. There were gingerbread men and chocolate logs, banana muffins and sugar mice. Katy licked her lips. Which cakes should they take to the party?

Suddenly Tim spotted a big notice. On it was a special message from the party pixie. It told them exactly which cakes to choose.

Can you find the party cakes?

Katy and Tim, please bring these cakes to the party.

1 of these

2 of these

3 of these

2 of these

yum yum

The toy shop

Next Katy and Tim headed for the toy shop. Here they found Mr Tedd, the owner, puzzling over a chart pinned to the counter.

"The party pixie has told me to wear one of these four costumes to the Puzzle Town party," Mr Tedd explained, pointing to the poster. "I'll work out which one by finding the only toy in my shop that matches one of these pictures. But is it the king, the ghost, the detective or the cowboy?"

Which costume will Mr Tedd wear to the party?

The party is beside a bridge.

9

A fruity puzzle

At the fruit and vegetable shop Katy and Tim looked at all the delicious things and wondered what to choose. Then Katy spotted a blackboard. It was another special message. Katy and Tim read it carefully. Now they knew exactly what fruit to buy. But there was a catch - every fruit had to be different.

What fruit should Tim and Katy choose?

The party is under a big clock.

Oranges

Katy and Tim
Please choose

3 green fruits

4 red fruits

2 yellow fruits

2 orange fruits

Remember - NO two fruits must be the same.

Apple Tree

Doughnut Tree

Whose shoes?

With the fruit in their bags, Tim and Katy skipped off to collect Katy's new sandals from the shoe shop. But the shop was in a dreadful mess, and none of the customers had any shoes on at all.

"I'll fetch your sandals in a minute, Katy," said Clive, the assistant. "But first I must find shoes for all these people."

Can you help Clive match the customers with their shoes?

13

Lots of letters

The Post Office was the last place on their list. Here Katy and Tim found three letter boxes, each for a different type of mail. Zippy mail was for urgent letters, Snail mail was for letters that weren't very important and Air mail was for letters going to another country. Tim and Katy read the Post Office notice board and looked at the stamps on their letters. They soon worked out what they had to do.

Which letters should go into which letter boxes?

Look carefully at your *stamps*.
Please put all your letters into the right letter boxes.

Zippy mail =
10 Puzzle Pennies

Snail mail =
5 Puzzle Pennies

Air mail =
15 Puzzle Pennies

PARCEL POST

Zippy

Zippy mail only = 10PP

Curious crossings

Now their errands were done, but Tim and Katy still hadn't found the party. Then Tim had a brainwave. They would ask their friend Molly, the mechanic at the Puzzle Town garage, what to do next. She knew everything.

Outside the Post Office, Katy and Tim saw they had to cross lots of roads to reach the garage. They knew the Puzzle Town Road Code - only cross at the striped crossings. But some of the crossings were blocked, so they couldn't cross at these.

Can you find a safe route to the garage using the clear crossings only?

Pirates rule

Treasure for ALL!

Horatio is innocent

Molly's Garage

The missing tool kit

At the garage, Katy and Tim found Molly looking for her lost tools. She had lots of Puzzle Town cars to mend.

"I'll help you on your way to the party, if you two help me find my missing tools," said Molly. "I've lost a screwdriver, a saw, a hammer, a light, a very big nail and my new red cleaning cloth."

Katy and Tim looked around the messy garage. It certainly wasn't going to be an easy job.

Can you find Molly's lost tools?

A puzzling procession

Molly smiled mysteriously. She told the children to follow the group with the most legs in the Puzzle Town procession. There were four groups to choose from - the jolly rollerskaters, the silly skateboards, the prancing ponies and the unusual unicyclists.

Katy and Tim were wondering what she meant, when suddenly they heard laughter and cheering. Racing outside they saw, to their surprise, a strange procession of people and animals. But which was the group with most legs? Then Tim gave a shout. He knew who to follow.

Which group should Tim and Katy follow?

The amazing maze

The prancing ponies led Katy and Tim to the Puzzle Town park. When they told the children there was something for them in the middle of the maze, Katy and Tim groaned. The maze was so big and twisty. Would they ever find their way to the middle, and out again?

Can you find the way to the middle of the maze?

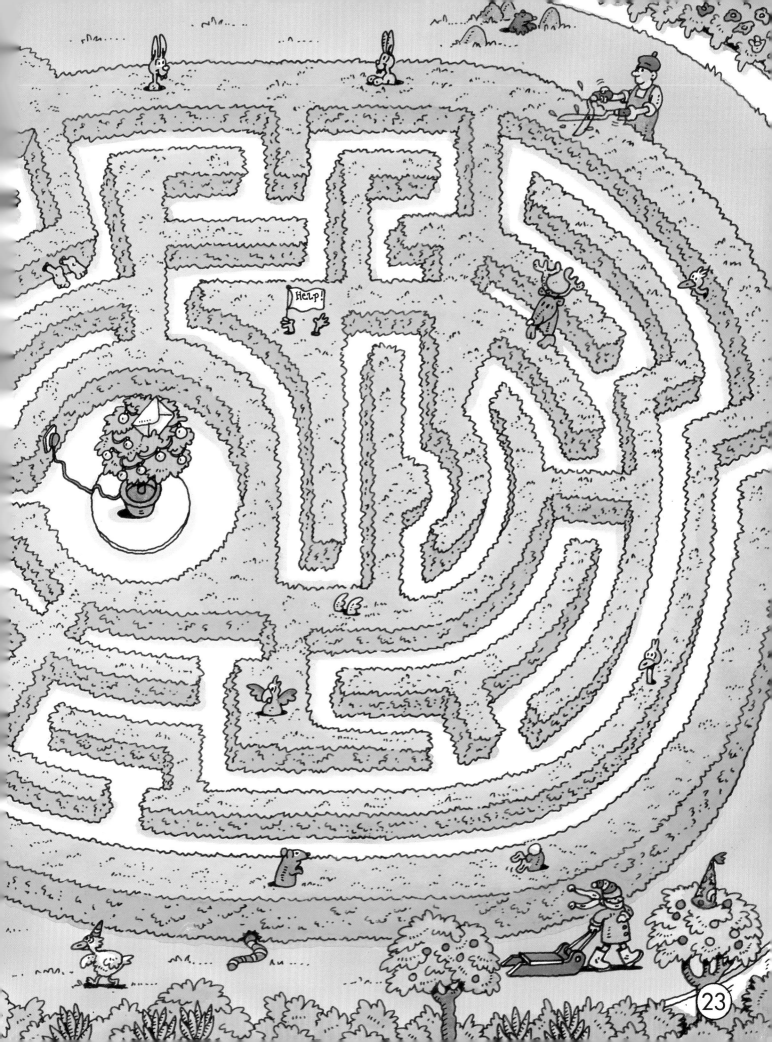

Map reading

In the middle of the maze, Katy and Tim found an envelope addressed to them. Inside was their party invitation and a message from the party pixie, listing the five clues they had already found. There was also a map, showing the other side of Puzzle Town.

"Now we can find the party," said Katy.

Look at all the clues again. Then look at the map. Where is the party being held?

Katy and Tim
are invited to the Puzzle Town party
today at 3pm.

 You will find the party next to three tall trees.

 The party is beside a bridge.

 The party is under a big clock.

 The party is in a street that begins with an 'S'.

 The party is outside a brown building. (It doesn't look like this one).

The above five clues will help you find the Puzzle Town party on the map.

Dear Katy and Tim,
Before you go to the Puzzle Town party, please
collect the party guests from Puzzle Town Station.
Love from the Party Pixie ×××

At the station

At last Katy and Tim knew where the party was. But first they had to rush to Puzzle Town station.

"The party guests have arrived," called Joe the guard. "They're waiting for you on the party train."

"Which one is it?" asked Katy.

"It has a green engine, or is it blue? I know it's got spots and is driven by engineer Emma," Joe said.

Can you find the Puzzle Town party train?

Puzzle Town Station

The Puzzle Town party!

Katy and Tim led the way to the Puzzle Town party, followed by all their new friends. And what a party it was! There were cakes and clowns, jugglers and jellies, bubbles and balloons. Katy and Tim saw lots of familiar faces. Even the mysterious balloon thief was there. As for the party pixie, well he was already planning next year's Puzzle Town party.

How many party guests have you seen before?
Can you spot the balloon thief?

Odd things

Did you spot all the odd things going on in Puzzle Town? If not, go back and have another look. If you can't find them, here's a list of all the things Katy and Tim saw on their adventure.

Pages	Odd things
4-5	Sea monster, tiger on a swing, twisty chimney, broken broom handle, duck in boots, the flower shop door is in a strange place!
6-7	Broken chair leg, upside-down teapot spout, a polar bear eating a biscuit, sausages hanging from roof.
8-9	Pickled onions, web-footed doll, aliens, boy with one bare foot.
10-11	Giant legs at crossing, broken trolley handle, duck, tree trunk, doughnut tree.
12-13	Chicks in a box, shoe box full of bananas, child with boot on head, duck in boots.
14-15	Alien photos, parcelled elephant, parcelled snake.
16-17	Ballet-dancing hippo, giraffe in car, monster in pond.
18-19	Dog mechanic, three-wheeled car, snake hose, flowers in exhaust.
20-21	Giraffe in house, feet in roof, dog taking man for a walk.
22-23	Person dressed for winter, upside-down boots, plug in hedge, bird wearing hat, man with three legs.
24-25	Animal with sunglasses, silly street names.
26-27	Tiger dressed as person, lady with upside-down umbrella, strange creatures, ice-skater, firebucket, man in skirt, boat sign.
28-29	What a strange party!

Answers

Pages 4-5
Setting off

These are the shops that Katy and Tim should go to.

Post Office — letters

Shoe shop — shoes

Fruit and vegetable shop — fruit

Bakers — cakes

Toy shop — party hats

Pages 6-7
Lovely cakes

The cakes are circled in red.

Pages 8-9   The toy shop

The ghost is the only toy that appears in the shop and on the chart. So Mr Tedd must choose the ghost costume.

Pages 10-11   A fruity puzzle

You could choose several different combinations of fruit. But Katy and Tim chose these:
Green — apple, grape, lime; Red — cherry, plum, strawberry, rhubarb; Yellow — lemon, banana; Orange — peach, orange.

Pages 12-13
Whose shoes?

You can find the shoes and the feet they fit by matching the coloured circles shown here.

Pages 14-15
Lots of letters

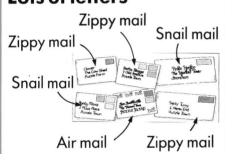

Zippy mail

Zippy mail

Snail mail

Snail mail

Air mail

Zippy mail

Pages 16-17   Curious crossings

The route across the clear crossings is marked in red.

Pages 18-19
The missing tools

Molly's missing tools are circled in red.

Pages 20-21
A puzzling procession

The prancing ponies are the group with the most legs in the procession.

Pages 22-23
The amazing maze

The way through the maze is marked in red.

Pages 24-25
Map reading

This is the place where the party is being held. It is the only place on the map that matches all the clues.

Pages 26-27
At the station

This is the Puzzle Town party train.

Pages 28-29
The Puzzle Town party!

This is the balloon thief.

Look back through the book and see if you can spot all the people who are now at the party.

Did you spot everything?
Fancy dress

The chart below shows you which piece of either Katy's or Tim's fancy dress costume is hidden on which double page. Katy's costume is a wizard, and Tim's is a clown.

Pages	Fancy dress
4-5	Magic kitten
6-7	Spell book
8-9	Joke flower
10-11	Wand
12-13	Striped socks
14-15	Slippers
16-17	Red nose
18-19	Cloak
20-21	Big shoes
22-23	Hat
24-25	Face paints
26-27	Funny wig

Balloon thief

Did you remember to look out for that naughty balloon thief? At least he brought the balloons to the party in the end!

This edition first published in 2003 by Usborne Publishing Ltd., Usborne House, 83-85 Saffron Hill, London EC1N 8RT, England.

www.usborne.com Copyright © 2003, 1991 Usborne Publishing Ltd.

The name Usborne and the devices ♀ ⊕ are Trade Marks of Usborne Publishing Ltd. All rights reserved. No part of this publication may be reproduced, stored in a retrieval system or transmitted in any form or by any means, electronic, mechanical, photocopying, recording or otherwise, without the prior permission of the publisher.

U.E. Printed in Portugal.